© Evie Jeang 2022

ISBN: 978-1-66782-005-7

eBook ISBN: 978-1-66782-006-4

How Much We Love You

Evie Jeang
Illustrated by Alex Spendlove

Untraditional Family Family: Book One

For Evan: My Son

mon petit prince

EVIE JEANG.

With two decades worth of experience, Evie has made it a career in helping families navigate their way through the family law courts in the State of California; as well as assisting couples through the intricate laws governing international surrogacy through in vitro fertilization, egg freezing, gestational surrogacy and more. Her entire life's work has been centered around family. This is the story of how she started hers.

As mommy and daddy were driving little Evan to his classmate, Alex's birthday party, mommy notice little Evan was staring at the widow from her rear mirror.

3

Little Evan: mommy, how do I come from your stomach when your stomach is so small and I am so much bigger?!"

Mommy laugh and say: you are right my little prince and you are too big to come out of mommy's stomach huh?
However, you know about manifestation? The special power that we have? Is when you really want something and we always picture how it would be or how it would look or see....

Well, mommy was dreaming about you and imagine how you will look and how cute of a boy you are going to be....so mommy send her intention out and an angel came and help mommy to have you?

Mommy: Oh yes...there is this angel and her name is Angel Elba.

9

so she came to mommy and told mommy that she will help me to protect you and bring you home to us

Mommy: Well.... mommy has this huge ball, like a size of grapefruit, in mommy's stomach so mommy don't have enough of space to have you in the stomach

so this angel decide to protect you and have you put in her stomach first until you are big and healthy enough to meet mommy and daddy.

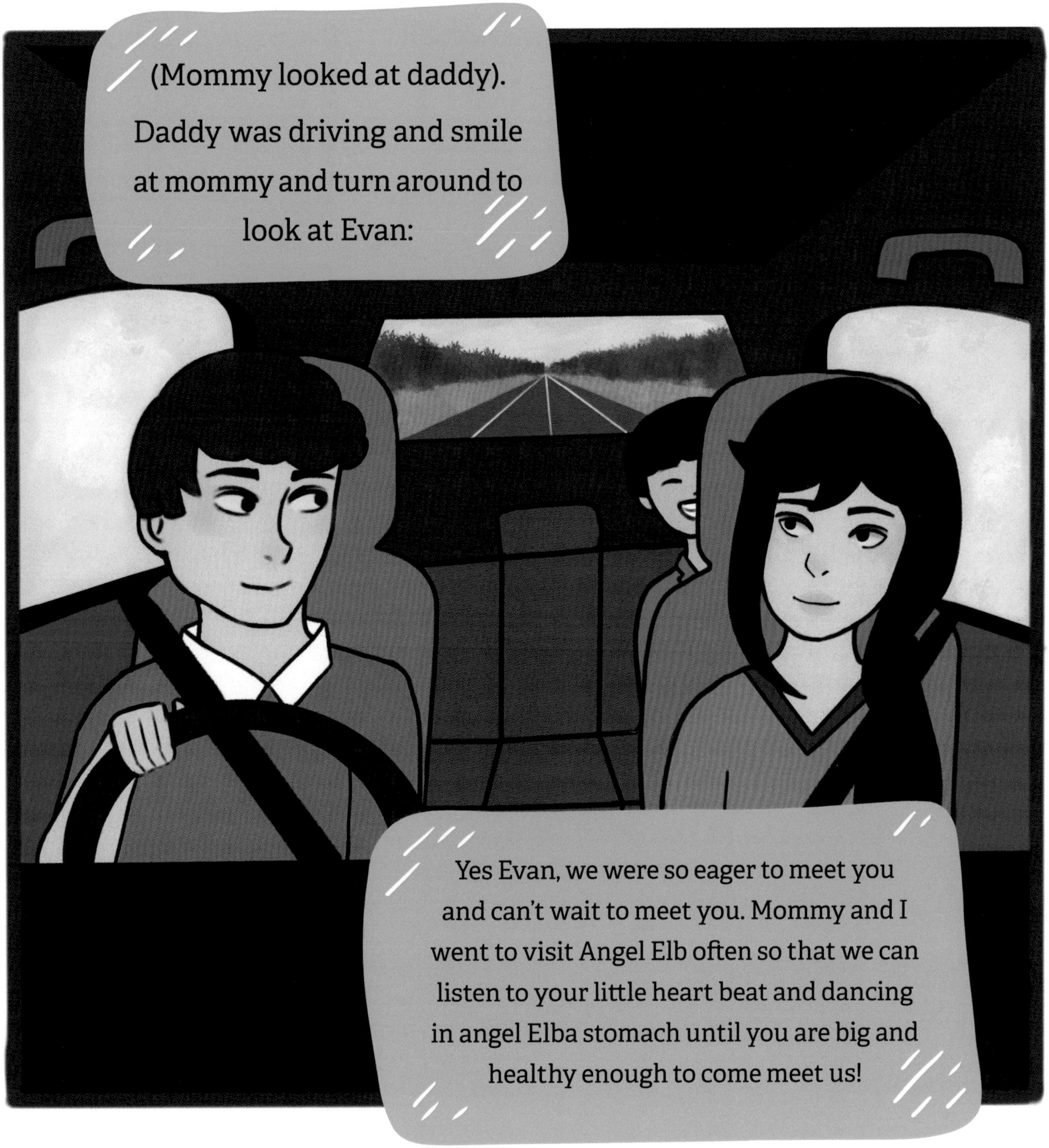
(Mommy looked at daddy). Daddy was driving and smile at mommy and turn around to look at Evan:
Yes Evan, we were so eager to meet you and can't wait to meet you. Mommy and I went to visit Angel Elb often so that we can listen to your little heart beat and dancing in angel Elba stomach until you are big and healthy enough to come meet us!

We even see you in the stomach smiling from this big screen when you were inside of Angel Elba's stomach.

Evan's eyes were big and bright....he seems very intrigue and suddenly his eyes wide up as seems he just has this light bulb on...and he says with size of excitement.. "
mommy, you are right, your stomach is too small to both fit me and a grapefruit size ball in your stomach."

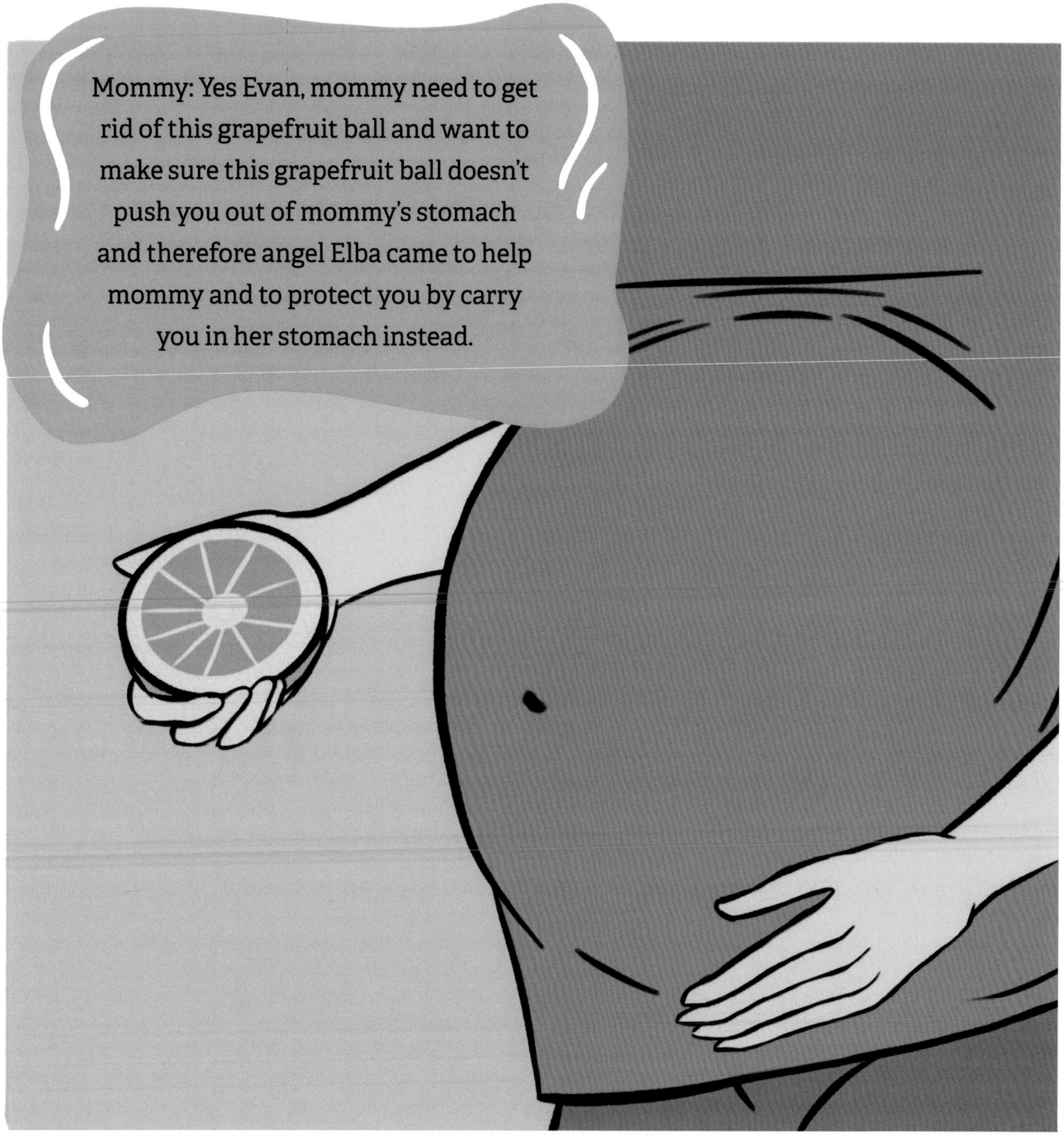
Mommy: Yes Evan, mommy need to get rid of this grapefruit ball and want to make sure this grapefruit ball doesn't push you out of mommy's stomach and therefore angel Elba came to help mommy and to protect you by carry you in her stomach instead.

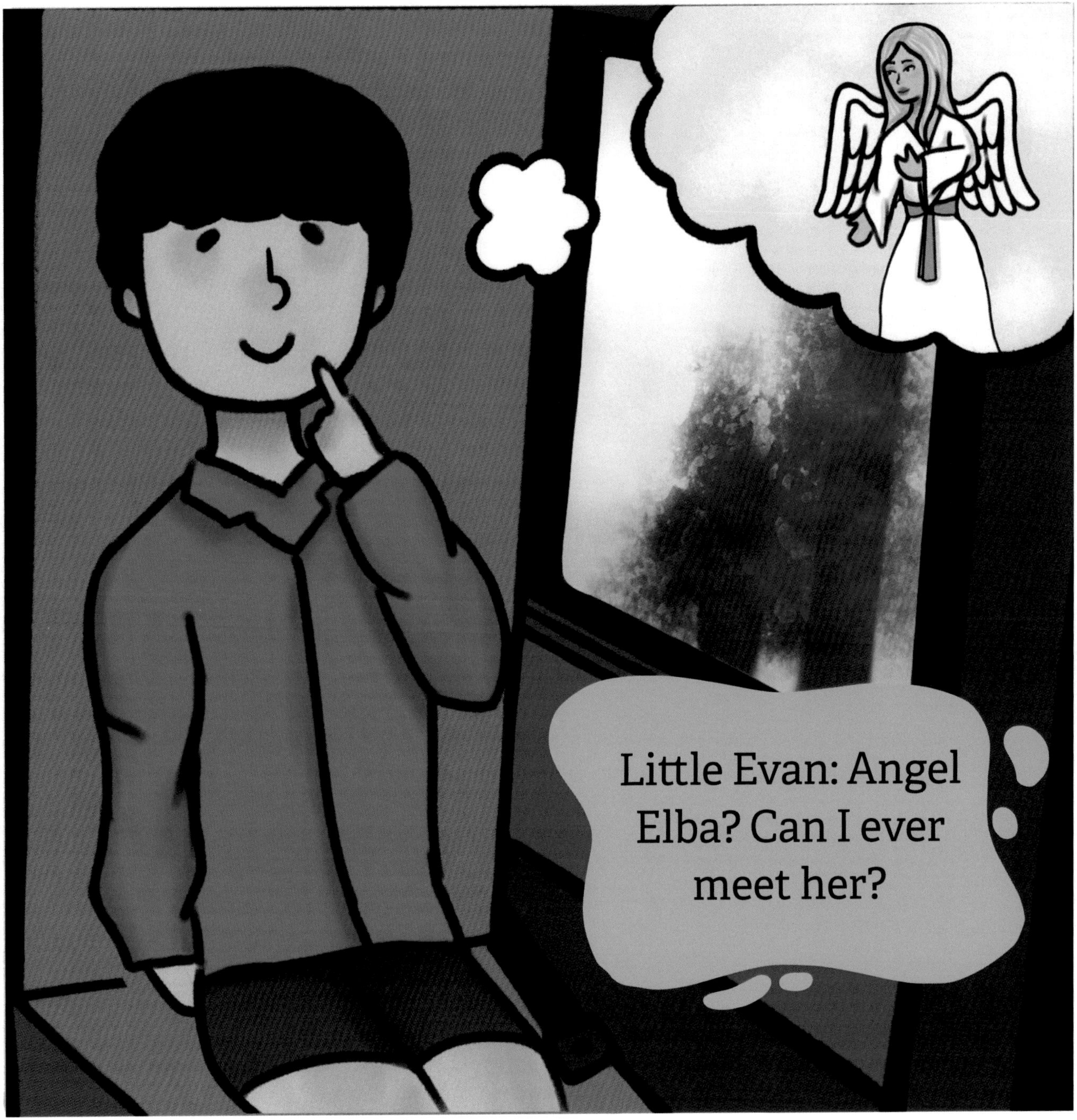
Little Evan: Angel Elba? Can I ever meet her?

Mommy: Oh yes, angel Elba talk to mommy often and always care about you. Would you like to meet her and her little boy? We can go meet her if you want...

Daddy laugh and look at mommy with the wink in his eye: Ok, we can go visit angel Elba and her little boy!